Our Physical World

# Temperature

by Rebecca Olien

**Consultant:**
Philip W. Hammer, PhD
Vice President, The Franklin Center
The Franklin Institute
Philadelphia, Pennsylvania

First Facts is published by Capstone Press
151 Good Counsel Drive, P.O. Box 669, Mankato, Minnesota 56002
www.capstonepress.com

*Library of Congress Cataloging-in-Publication Data*
Olien, Rebecca.
    Temperature / by Rebecca Olien.
        p. cm.—(First facts. Our physical world)
    Includes bibliographical references and index.
    Contents: Temperature—Changing temperatures—Melting and freezing—Heat moves—
Temperature and weather—Measuring temperature—Anders Celsius—Temperature
safety—Amazing but true!—Hands on: freezing solid.
        ISBN 0-7368-2619-X (hardcover)
        1. Temperature—Juvenile literature. [1. Temperature.] I. Title. II. Series.
QC271.4.O38 2005
536.5—dc22                                                          2003025828

Summary: Introduces temperature and provides instructions for an activity to demonstrate some
    of its characteristics.

**Editorial Credits**
Christopher Harbo, editor; Linda Clavel, series designer; Molly Nei, book designer;
    Scott Thoms, photo researcher; Eric Kudalis, product planning editor

**Photo Credits**
Bruce Coleman Inc./Ian & Karen Stewart, 10
Capstone Press/Gary Sundermeyer, cover, 5, 6–7, 9, 11, 14, 15
Comstock, 18–19
Dwight R. Kuhn, 20
Folio Inc./John Burwell, 8
Mary Evens Picture Library, 17
Tom Stack & Associates Inc./Mark Allen Stack, 13

1 2 3 4 5 6 09 08 07 06 05 04

# Table of Contents

# Temperature

Temperature tells people how hot or cold something is. People sometimes touch things to check temperature. Bread from the oven feels hot. Ice cream from the freezer feels cold. Some things are too hot or too cold to touch. People should be careful about what they touch.

# Changing Temperatures

Temperatures can change. Hot things are cooled by air and water. Cold things get warmer in sunlight or over a fire. A camper heats soup over a fire. The temperature of the soup rises. The soup **boils**.

 **Fun Fact!**
Yellowstone National Park has hot springs. These pools of water are heated by hot rock under the ground.

# Melting and Freezing

Temperature changes can make things change form. Hot temperatures can melt things. Butter melts on a hot ear of corn.

Cold temperatures can freeze things. Grape juice changes from a liquid to a solid in the freezer. Frozen juice makes a good treat.

## Heat Moves

Heated air **expands** and rises. A hot air balloon heats air with burners. The hot air lifts the balloon into the sky.

Heat travels through **conductors**. Metal is a good conductor of heat. A metal spoon warms up in hot chocolate.

# Temperature and Weather

Temperatures change the weather. Sunlight heats the air. Thunderstorms can happen when warm, wet air meets cool, dry air. Rain changes to snow or ice when temperatures drop below the freezing point.

13

# Measuring Temperature

Thermometers are tools that measure temperature. Thermometers can measure the temperatures of air, food, and people.

Thermometers use **Fahrenheit** (F) and **Celsius** (C) **scales** to measure temperature. These scales help people know how hot or cold something is.

# Anders Celsius

Anders Celsius was a Swedish scientist in the early 1700s. He studied math and space. He created the Celsius temperature scale. On this scale, water freezes at 0 degrees Celsius. Water boils at 100 degrees Celsius. The Celsius scale is used in most countries.

**Fun Fact!**
The United States uses the Fahrenheit scale. Daniel Gabriel Fahrenheit made this scale in the early 1700s.

17

# Temperature Safety

People stay safe in different temperatures. They wear light clothes and hats to keep cool in hot weather. They wear warm hats and mittens to stay warm in cold weather.

 **Fun Fact!**
Divers wear dry suits to explore lakes and oceans in winter. A dry suit keeps a diver's body heat in and cold water out.

19

# Amazing but True!

The North American wood frog freezes nearly solid in winter. In its arctic home, the frog goes into a deep winter sleep. Its breathing and heartbeat slow to a stop. Much of its body freezes solid. In spring, the wood frog's body thaws. Its breathing and heartbeat restart.

# Hands On: Freezing Solid

You can make ice pops by freezing fruit juice. Measure how long it takes juice to freeze solid in your freezer.

## What You Need

small paper cup
fruit juice
plastic spoon
paper
pencil

## What You Do

1. Fill the paper cup ¾ full of juice. Put a plastic spoon in the cup. Put the cup in the freezer.
2. After 30 minutes, check the juice in the cup. On a piece of paper, write down what the juice looks like. Is it frozen yet? Can the spoon still move in the cup?
3. Put the cup back in the freezer.
4. Continue checking the juice every 30 minutes. Each time, write down what the juice looks like. How much time does it take the juice to freeze solid?
5. When the juice has frozen solid, peel away the paper cup and enjoy your frozen treat.

# Glossary

boil (BOIL)—to heat a liquid until it begins to bubble and give off steam

Celsius (SEL-see-uhss)—a scale for measuring temperature; water freezes at 0 degrees Celsius.

conductor (kuhn-DUHK-tur)—a material that lets heat, electricity, or sound travel easily through it; metal is a good conductor of heat.

expand (ek-SPAND)—to increase in size

Fahrenheit (FA-ren-hite)—a scale for measuring temperature; water freezes at 32 degrees Fahrenheit.

scale (SKALE)—a series of numbers used to measure something

# Read More

**Richardson, Adele.** *Thermometers.* First Facts. Science Tools. Mankato, Minn.: Capstone Press, 2004.

**Royston, Angela.** *Hot and Cold.* My World of Science. Chicago: Heinemann, 2002.

# Internet Sites

FactHound offers a safe, fun way to find Internet sites related to this book. All of the sites on FactHound have been researched by our staff.

Here's how:
1. Visit *www.facthound.com*
2. Type in this special code **073682619X** for age-appropriate sites. Or enter a search word related to this book for a more general search.
3. Click on the **Fetch It** button.

FactHound will fetch the best sites for you!

# Index